VETERINARIAN,
Doctor for Your Pet

VETERINARIAN,

Doctor for Your Pet

Text and Pictures by

Arline Strong

Atheneum · New York · 1979

To my friend Mary Macdonald

Dr. Barbara R. Strauss is a member of the Westchester-Rockland Veterinary Medical Association.

Library of Congress Cataloging in Publication Data

Strong, Arline.
   Veterinarian.

   SUMMARY: Introduces the work of a veterinarian especially in preventing and treating diseases in animals.
   1. Veterinarians—Juvenile literature.
[1. Veterinarians. 2. Occupations] I. Title.
SF756.S76   636.089'023   76–46948
ISBN 0–689–10781–1

VETERINARIAN,
Doctor for Your Pet

BARBARA STRAUSS is a Doctor of Veterinary Medicine. To prepare for her work, she studied for many years at a school of veterinary medicine. Although she learned to care for many kinds of animals, she specializes in the care and treatment of companion animals. Most of these are cats and dogs, although occasionally a hamster, rabbit or bird may be brought to her office.

Animals are brought to Dr. Strauss for many reasons: treatment of injuries or illness; immunization to diseases; need for surgery or dentistry; and routine checkups. Some are new pets. A new cat or dog may have been received as a gift, purchased from a kennel, a breeder or shop, adopted from a shelter or found somewhere. No matter what its origin, veterinarians usually advise an initial checkup.

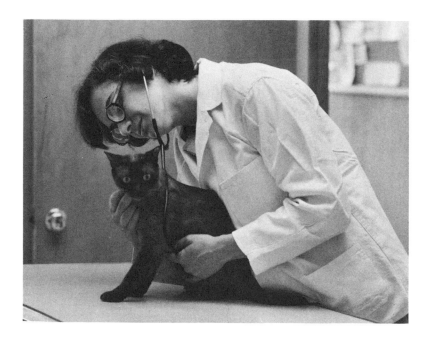

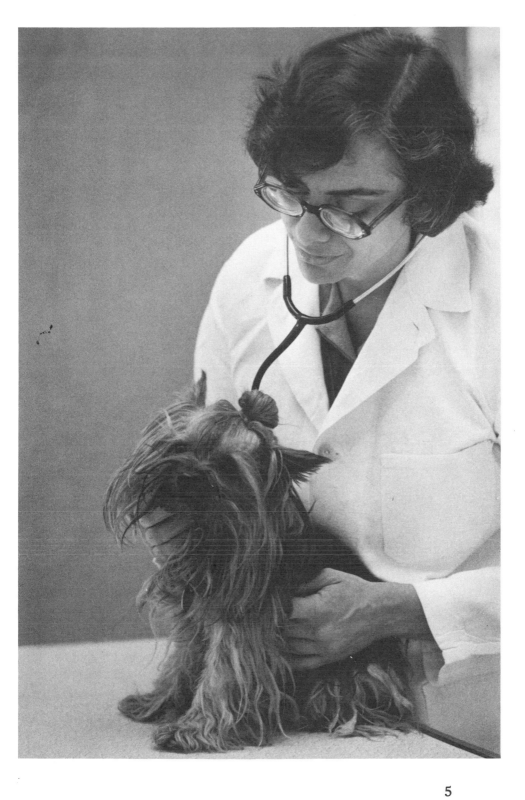

Appointments are scheduled as accurately as possible so the patients and their owners have little time to wait in the reception room. The time goes by fast, however, because it is fun to watch the variety of animals. Owners usually enjoy exchanging stories about their pets' personalities and problems.

The receptionist, Terry Cahn, greets the patients and their owners. She asks the reasons for their visits and records the information for the doctor.

Some animals are very interested in other patients.

Some find the reception room a cozy place to relax, and others seem more anxious to be on their way out.

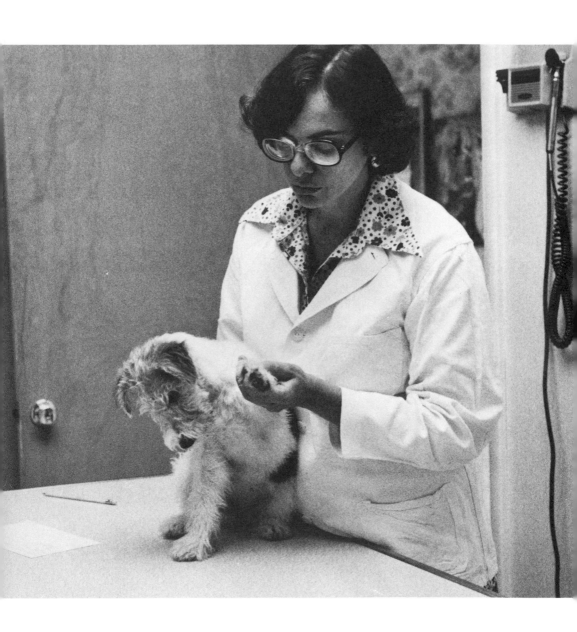

The owner who brings a new puppy or kitten to a veterinarian may be unaware of how many different aspects of health are being examined while the animal is there.

The mouth is checked. Kittens and puppies develop two sets of teeth just as human children do.

Various birth defects can be discovered or ruled out by listening to the heart and lungs with a stethoscope.

Eyes need to be checked, and so do ears. Parasites known as ear mites, for example, can easily be detected and treated; but if they are neglected, they can cause infections and complications.

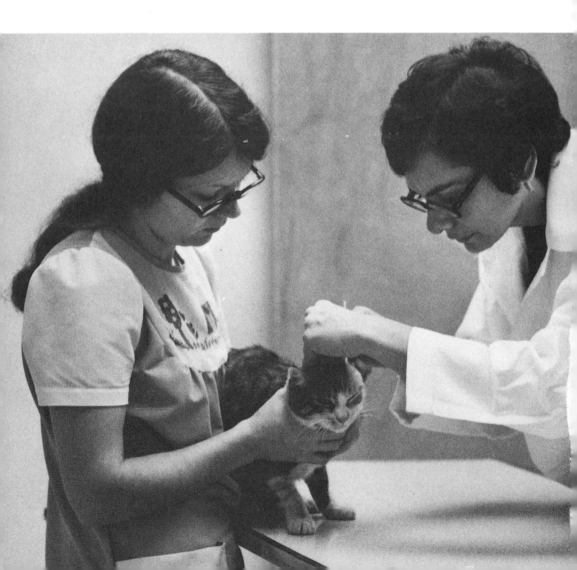

When Dr. Strauss seems to be idly stroking a pet's fur, chances are she is also checking for fleas, ticks, rashes or fungus infections.

While seeming to be only sociable, the doctor is also observing behavior and noting general conformation.

Most likely, a new pet will be found in good health. Then it takes a discussion of proper care and diet to get it off to a good start.

Preventive medicine is the ideal way to keep a pet healthy. Vaccines protect animals against specific future illnesses. Dogs receive injections against canine distemper, hepatitis, leptospirosis and rabies. Cats are protected from feline distemper and also against rabies if they go outdoors. There are also vaccines available against some of the respiratory viruses that affect cats, which some veterinarians recommend.

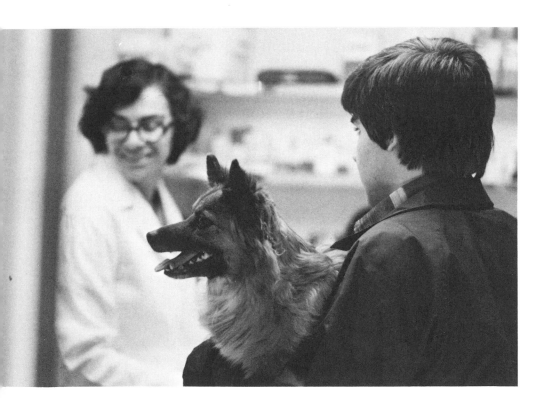

Being taken for their first checkup is just
another game to three little kittens.

The doctor uses a light to examine ears, and
Chino uses his nose to investigate the light.

Dr. Strauss gets a good look at Mishu's eyes.

And then takes an extra minute to make friends with her new patient.

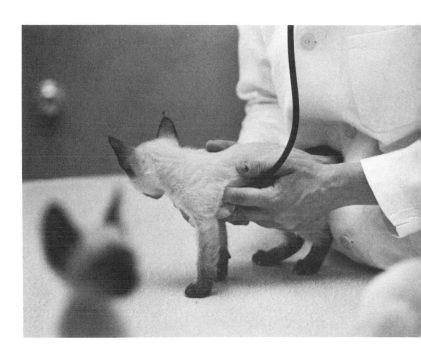

Tiki's heart and lungs sound fine.

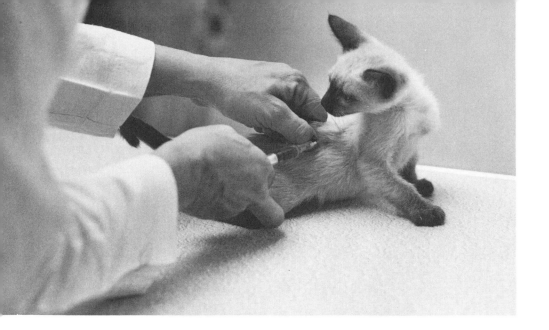

An injection is given so quickly that Dr. Strauss does not need an assistant to hold a kitten the size of Mishu.

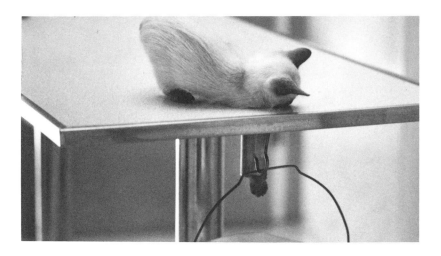

It didn't hurt a bit. A moment later, Mishu is more interested in exploring the new surroundings.

Chino is offered his first taste of vitamins.

Dr. Strauss begins a medical history for the kittens. She records important facts: the dates that vaccines were given, weight, and even the kittens' birth date. It's not unusual for owners to forget the ages of their pets in later years.

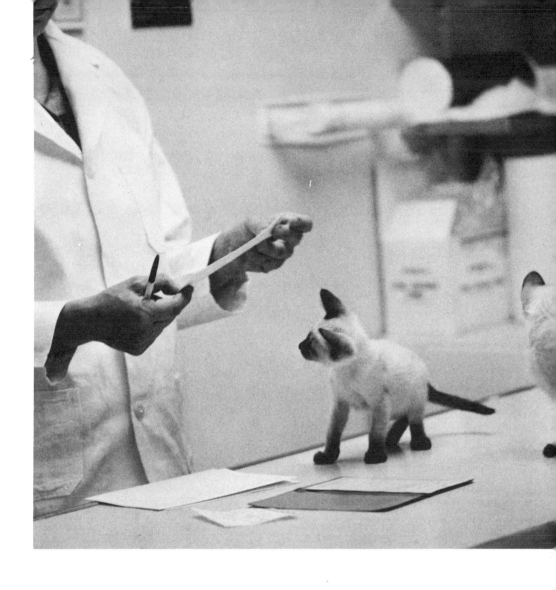

Instructions for care are written on the back of
the card given to the owner of the kittens. Dr.
Strauss recommends a diet that does not
include bones, fish, pork or spices. Copies of all
medical records are kept in the office for future
reference.

Extra vitamins and minerals are recommended for young growing animals, for older animals and pregnant animals. Sometimes, doctors also recommend vitamins for other animals. Even a pet that eats large quantities of food does not always get a well-balanced diet and may benefit from some extra vitamins.

Dr. Strauss encourages owners to call her for advice if they have problems with their pets. Some medicines that are good for humans may be harmful to animals. Some are good for one type of animal but not for another. Aspirin, for example, can be toxic to cats.

In her animal clinic, Dr. Strauss schedules surgery after the morning office hours. Since it is the first few hours following an operation that are critical, she and her technician, Gloria Hudson, can then observe the animal's postoperative progress all afternoon.

An animal having surgery is put to sleep with an anesthetic. The anesthetic prevents it from feeling any pain during the operation. Soon after the surgery, the anesthetic wears off and the animal will probably be awake for a while. Later, when the office is closed and quiet, the patient will sleep through the night.

Animals most often need surgery for the setting of fractured bones, removal of tumors, treatment of lacerations or wounds, removal of foreign bodies from the throat, stomach or intestinal tract, dentistry and neutering.

Neutering is also known as *altering* a male or *spaying* a female cat or dog. The reproductive organs are removed so the animal cannot become a parent. The operation is safe and humane.

Pet owners often ask Dr. Strauss whether they should neuter their pets or not. A litter of kittens or puppies can be a houseful of fun, but the pleasure can be spoiled if new homes cannot be found for the babies as they grow older.

There are always some people looking for new pets, but too many kittens and puppies mean that some will be unwanted and maybe uncared for. This is something everyone should think about before they let their pets breed. Another factor in favor of spaying is that female cats and dogs that are spayed before their first heat never develop breast tumors. Of course, breeding can also be avoided by preventing females in heat or unaltered males from wandering free.

Dentistry is an important part of health care for pets. A pet may need to have oral surgery or may simply need to have its teeth cleaned.

A veterinarian or pet owner can easily decide if teeth need to be cleaned by simply looking at them. If a brown deposit called tartar is present, the teeth need to be cleaned. If tartar is allowed to remain too long, it will accumulate under the gums and cause the roots of teeth to decay. If the roots of a tooth are destroyed, the animal will lose the tooth.

Some pets may never need their teeth cleaned. Others may need it done often or only on rare occasions.

Few alert cats or dogs are willing to let a veterinarian work on their teeth, even if the work is just a painless cleaning. A light anesthetic or tranquilizer may be needed so that the animal will be too drowsy to object.

The injection of anesthetic will not hurt, but
even a gentle dog might be startled by it, and
instinctively try to bite in self-defense. Gloria
holds Rudy until the anesthetic takes effect and
he is quiet. Dr. Strauss will then be
concentrating on the job of cleaning, and it is
important for Gloria to stand by to watch
Rudy's vital signs while he is under anesthesia.

An instrument known as an oral speculum is used to keep Rudy's mouth open so that even the inside of the back teeth can be reached.

Dr. Strauss carefully scrapes the tartar from each tooth.

Jeffrey, a golden retriever, has had surgery performed on his ear. His owner has brought him back to Dr. Strauss for an office visit. Some dogs, like Jeffrey, have drooping ears. Other dogs have ears that stand straight up or lie back when the dogs are relaxed. The position of the ear flaps on long-eared dogs makes it more difficult to notice or prevent ear problems.

Jeffrey has an ear infection. The infection was so annoying to the dog that he tried to relieve the discomfort by shaking his head.

He probably once shook his head too hard and caused a swelling of blood, known as a hematoma, to develop in his ear.

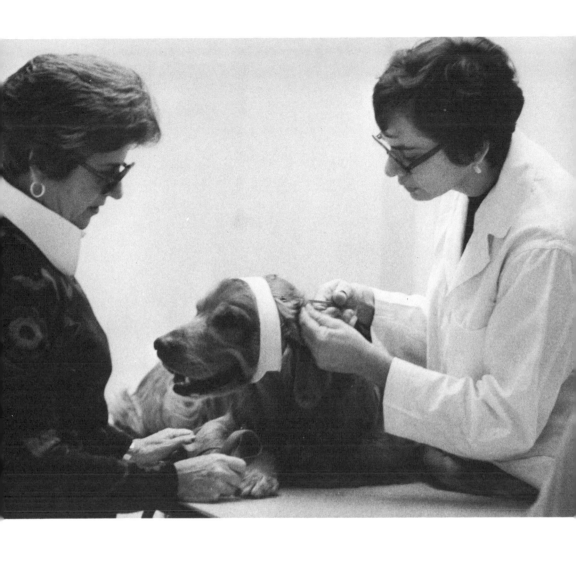

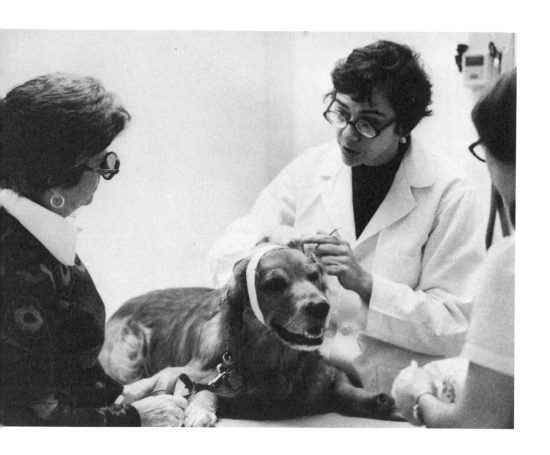

Dr. Strauss operated and removed the hematoma during Jeffrey's last visit. His owner has returned to the office with her dog to have his bandage changed.

When Jeffrey goes home, his owner will try to keep the new bandage dry. She will also continue to treat the infection with antibiotics until it is cured.

Veterinarians advise that all dog owners protect their pets against canine heartworm disease. Although it is not common to other animals and never a danger to people, the disease is dangerous to a dog's health.

It is much easier to prevent heartworm disease than it is to cure it. Heartworms are parasites. The infection can only be spread by mosquitoes. If a mosquito bites a dog that is infected with heartworms, that mosquito can carry the disease and give it to a healthy dog.

There is preventive medication that may be given to dogs. However, the preventive medication should not be given to a dog if it already has heartworm disease.

Before the beginning of the mosquito season, owners bring their dogs to Dr. Strauss for a blood test.

Dr. Strauss takes a small sample of blood. It doesn't hurt, but Gloria always holds a patient if there is a chance that it might be startled.

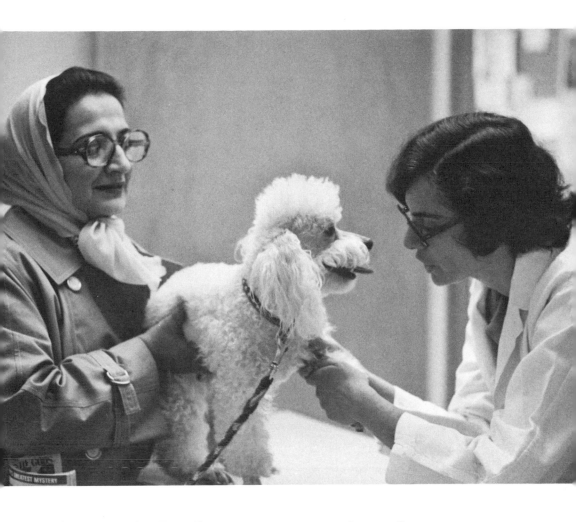

Afterwards, Dr. Strauss presses a piece of alcohol-soaked cotton against the area from which the blood was drawn, to prevent further bleeding.

Dr. Strauss writes instructions for use of the medicine. Before giving it to the dog, his owner will call the veterinarian's office to get the results of the blood test. If the dog is infected with heartworms, he will be treated for the disease. If all is well, the dog will be given the preventive medicine.

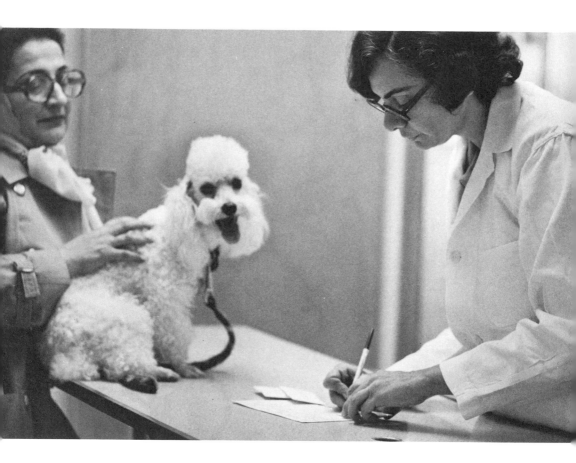

The dog's blood sample will be examined under the microscope for evidence of heartworms. The microscope is also used for blood counts, urinalysis, examination of skin scrapings for external parasites and fungus infections, and fecal analysis for intestinal parasites.

Gloria checks a cat's urine specimen with a color-coded strip of paper. The results will give the doctor clues to the cat's health.

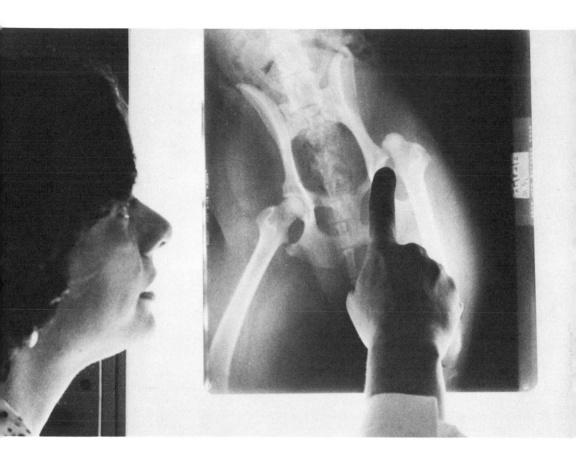

Radiographs are used to diagnose various
internal problems such as fractures or the
location of foreign bodies.

It does not require lab tests to understand this dog's problem. He has one of the most common complaints known to dogs: Fleas.

A dog that is allergic to flea bites will often seem to be scratching all the time. The constant itching bothers the dog. Although scratching doesn't really help, it is the only way that a dog can try to solve the problem by itself. Pets that have fleas need help from their owners.

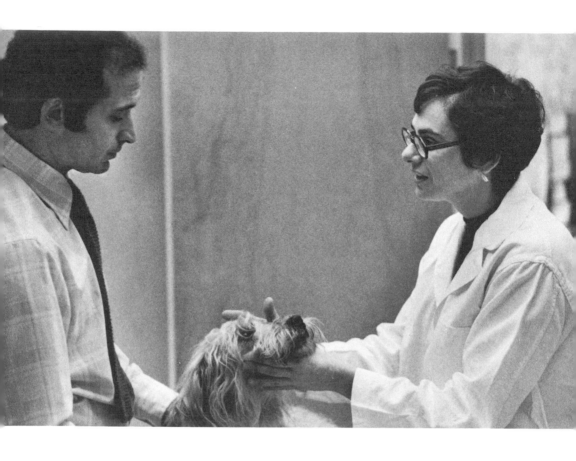

When pet owners cannot solve the problem, they usually ask a veterinarian for advice. Some dogs scratch so much that they develop sores on their skin. Dr. Strauss recommends a special bath and other medication to kill the fleas and relieve the itching.

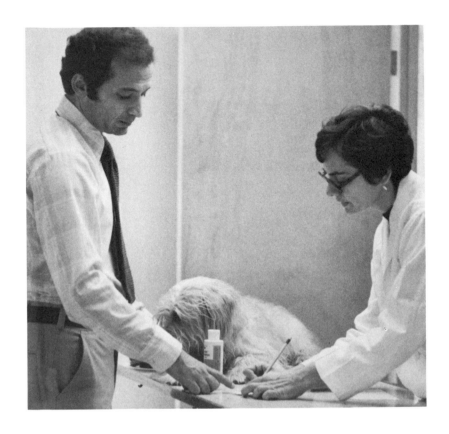

If a pet has fleas, then there are probably more fleas and flea eggs in their living quarters. Veterinarians advise treating the pet and the living quarters to get rid of all the fleas at one time.

Although a veterinarian is busy all day in
the office taking care of animals in these and
other ways, this is not all an animal doctor must
do. Dr. Strauss goes to seminars and reads
about new discoveries and treatments, so she
can be of the greatest help to her patients.
Being a veterinarian, like being a doctor for
people, is a job that takes specialized
knowledge, constant work and a love of living
creatures.

Glossary

Allergic	reacting unpleasantly to a substance which is inhaled, contacted or eaten
Antibiotic	a chemical substance that will kill bacteria or prevent their growth and multiplication
Blood count	analysis of the number and kind of red blood cells and white blood cells in a blood sample
Conformation	the formation and arrangement of the parts of the animal
Decay	to rot or deteriorate

Fecal Analysis	an examination of a stool specimen
Fungus	a group of many different types of plants that are parasites
Heat	the period of time during which a female animal is willing and able to mate
Infection	a disease caused by organisms that invade the body
Injection	the introduction of a liquid into some part of the body by means of a hypodermic needle
Laceration	a cut
Oral	the mouth
Parasite	an organism that lives on or in another kind of animal in order to obtain food or protection
Radiograph	an X-ray picture
Respiratory	involving the *respiratory system:* nose, throat, trachea, bronchial tubes and lungs

Tartar	a hard deposit on the teeth, consisting of saliva, proteins, food deposits and various mineral salts
Toxic	poisonous, or containing poison
Tranquilizer	a medication to soothe or calm
Tumor	an unnatural growth on or in some part of the body
Urinalysis	a study of a urine sample
Vaccine	a special preparation of either dead or weakened live micro-organisms that, when injected, helps the body become immune to certain diseases
Virus	a very tiny living substance that is too small to be seen by an ordinary microscope and that may cause illness